Meet My MISSISSIPPI

Illustrated by Brenda Ragsdale

Poem by

Patricia Neely~Dorsey

Copyright © 2013 by Patricia Neely-Dorsey

Illustrated by Brenda Ragsdale

All rights reserved. No part of this publication may be reproduced, distributed, or transmitted in any form or by any means, including photocopying, recording, or other electronic or mechanical methods, without the prior written permission of the publisher, except in the case of brief quotations embodied in critical reviews and certain other noncommercial uses permitted by copyright law.

ISBN: 978-1-7320846-8-1

Liberation's Publishing LLC
West Point, Mississippi
www.liberationspublishing.com

William Faulkner's Sanctuary

Eudora Welty's home state

Elvis Presley's birthplace

The bulk of the Natchez Trace

Choctaw Nation native land, Rolling hills of the Chickasaw band

Sprawling beaches

8

along the Gulf Coast shore

One blues man's Crossroads

And inspiration for more

Like Albert, B.B., Bukka, Howlin' Wolf, Little Milton, and Muddy Waters

who came to the fore

There's farm raised catfish, Delta tamales, seafood galore

14

and warm front porch welcomes with a wide-open door

Creative muse for Barq's™, Stetson™

Peavey™, Viking™

and Henson's famous green frog

and "Where the Southern Crosses the Yellow Dog"

An abundance

tradition

and folklore

with Ruins of Windsor

Vicksburg Battlefield

25

Emerald Mound

And Pharr Mounds to explore

27

You'll find an authentic Dentzel Carousel merry go round

Where Jimmie Rodgers fathered a unique country sound

She's the place where Coca Cola™ was bottled for the very first time   30

And Pine-Sol™ invented to combat dirt and grime

31

She's a ride down the Mighty River on the American Queen

and some of the most beautiful countryside that you've ever seen

She's music and melodies

And the mocking bird's songs

By valor and arms

and faith ever strong

She's magnolias blooming

around Jackson's capitol dome

with the buzz of the honeybee and sweet scent of the honeysuckle

that forever say "home"

Since December 10, 1817

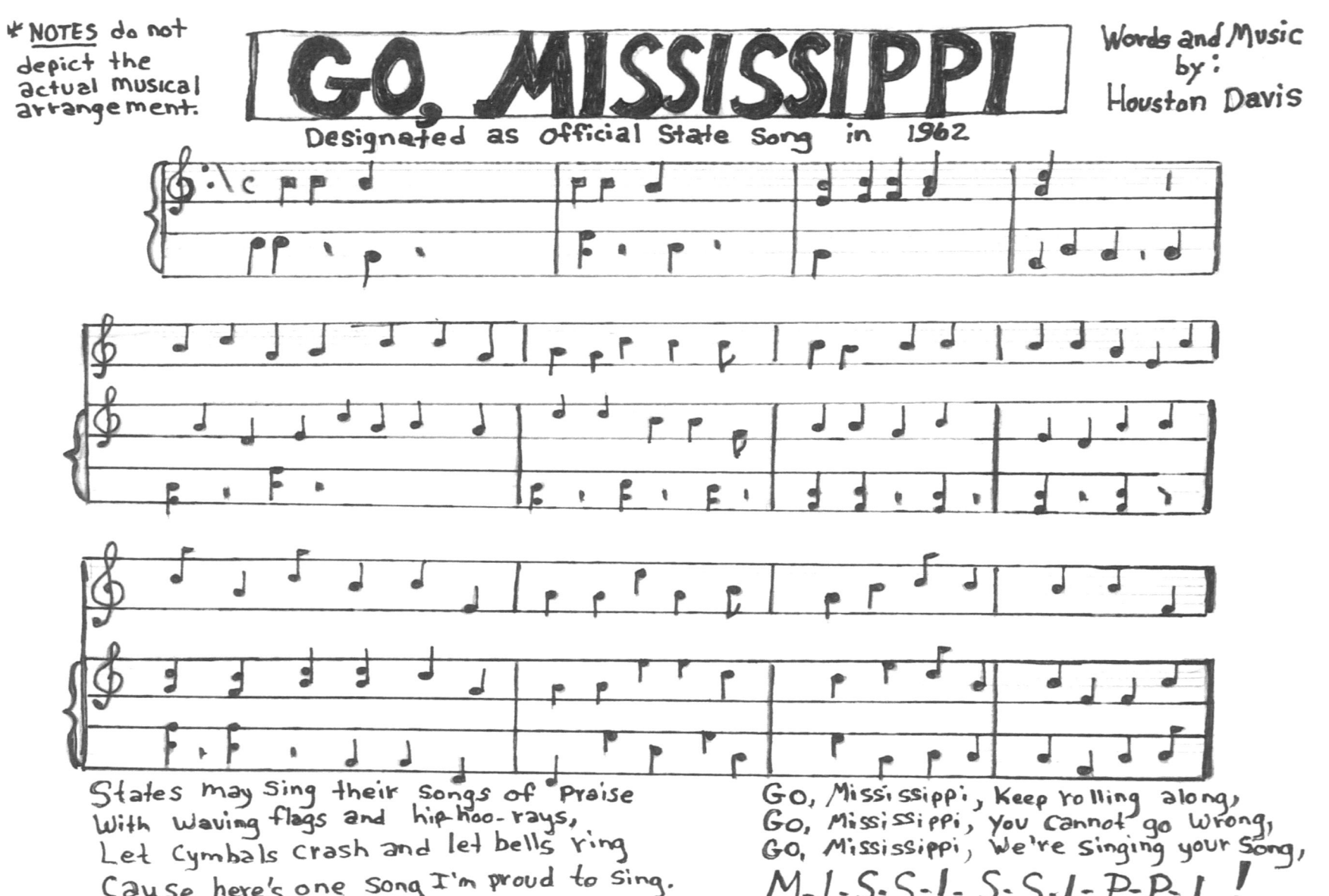

"Go Mississippi"

Roll on Mississippi

You're a true state of grace

MEET MY MISSISSIPPI

William Faulkner's Sanctuary
Eudora Welty's home state
Elvis Presley's birthplace
The bulk of the Natchez Trace;
Choctaw Nation native land
Rolling hills of the Chickasaw band
Sprawling beaches along the Gulf Coast shore
One blues man's Crossroads and inspiration for more;
Like Albert, B.B., Bukka, Howlin' Wolf ,
Little Milton and Muddy Waters who came to the fore
There's farm raised catfish , Delta tamales ,seafood galore
And warm front porch welcomes with a wide open door
Creative muse for Barq's™, Stetson™, Peavey™, Viking™
And Henson's famous green frog
And "Where The Southern Crosses The Yellow Dog "
An abundance of history, tradition and folklore
With Ruins of Windsor, Vicksburg Battlefield
Emerald Mound and Pharr Mounds to explore

You'll find an authentic Dentzel carousel merry go round
Where Jimmie Rodgers fathered a unique country sound
She's the place where Coca Cola™ was bottled for the very first time
And Pine-Sol™ invented to combat dirt and grime
She's a ride down the Mighty River on the American Queen
And some of the most beautiful countryside that you've ever seen
She's music and melodies and the mockingbird's songs,
By valor and arms and faith ever strong;
She's magnolias blooming around Jackson's capitol dome
With the buzz of the honeybee
And sweet scent of the honeysuckle
That forever say "home"
Since December 10, 1817
Our 20th state
"Go Mississippi "
The Hospitality State
Roll On Mississippi
You're a true state of grace.
Patricia Neely-Dorsey

Mississippi Trivia

Page 14: Mississippi is the leading producer of farm raised catfish in the U.S.

Page 20: The Mississippi Civil Rights Museum is the first state sponsored Civil rights museum in the country.

Page 21: The Old Capitol was restored and opened in 1961 as the state historical museum. The building is a National Historic Landmark.

Page 24: Windsor Ruins (23 Corinthian Columns) of the largest antebellum home in Mississippi built in 1861 and destroyed by fire in 1890. Windsor Ruins are located 12 miles from Port Gibson on Mississippi Highway 552.

Page 30: The Biedenharn Coca-Cola Museum houses a reproduction of the equipment first used to bottle Coca-Cola and a variety of Coca-Cola memorabilia.

Page 35: The Mockingbird is Mississippi's state bird.

Page 36: Mississippi's State Motto: virtute et armis

Page 37: The Great Seal of Mississippi was adopted in 1796 when Mississippi was still a U.S. Territory. In God we Trust was added in 2014.

Page 38: The Magnolia is Mississippi's state tree and state flower.
Jackson is the state's capital and largest city.

Page 40: Mississippi's state insect is the Honey Bee.

Page 46: The Governor's Mansion was designated a National Historic Landmark in 1975.

Page 47: Longwood Natchez Longwood Plantation, 30,000 sq. ft. is the largest octagonal house in the U.S. Longwood was designated a National Historic Landmark in 1971.

MEET MY MISSISSIPPI STUDY GUIDE

1. Mississippi has a rich literary history.

    A. Name the acclaimed Mississippi born writers mentioned in the poem along with birthplace and date.
    B. List their best known literary works and awards.
    C. Name at least five additional famous Mississippi born writers along with the same documentation.

2. Mississippi has a rich music history Mississippi has been called the Birthplace of America's Music.

    A. Name 3 different genres of music represented in the poem and a musician representative of that genre mentioned in the poem.
    B. List three facts about each of the representatives.

3. Mississippi has been called the Birthplace of The Blues

    A. Discuss the origins of this genre of music. List the famous Mississippi born blues musicians mentioned in the poem along with birthplace and date.
    B. List at least two facts about each one of the blues musicians.
    C. List at least two of their best-known works.

4. The Mississippi Delta

    A. Pinpoint the location of the Delta region of Mississippi
    B. List the counties included in the Mississippi Delta.
    C. Name three prominent cities/towns in the Delta and what each is best known for. Name three products that the Mississippi Delta is known for and why Name three other major regions of Mississippi and what they are known for.

5. The Natchez Trace
    A. Discuss the origins of the Natchez Trace and the groups and circumstances which led to its usage.
    B. Draw a map showing the course of the Trace. Name the city where the headquarters of the Natchez Trace Parkway is located.

6. Mississippi has a strong Native American history.

A. Name the Native American tribes which inhabited Mississippi with some facts about their location and lifestyle. List at least 10 Mississippi cities or counties with Native American names.
B. Discuss the significance of the Native American mounds mentioned in the poem along with their locations.
C. Name at least three other mounds and their locations.

7. Mississippi is a place that has fostered life changing and culture changing inventions and innovations.

   A. Name three Mississippi innovations or inventions mentioned in the poem.
   B. Give three facts about the inventions or innovations.
   C. Name at least 5 additional Mississippi inventions or innovations with date and locations.

8. Name three Mississippi National Landmarks mentioned in the poem

   A. Indicate location and when established as a historic landmark
   B. List three facts about the landmark.

9. Mississippi gets its name from the mighty Mississippi River which runs along its border.

   A. Give the Native American meaning of the name Mississippi
   B. List three facts about the Mississippi river.
   C. Draw a map showing the path of the Mississippi river with bordering states.

10. Name the Mississippi emblems and symbols mentioned in the poem
    A. Name when established as a state symbol / emblem
    B. State Bird State Flower, State Tree, State Capitol, State Insect, State Song.

VOCABULARY WORDS

sanctuary

bulk

inspiration

fore

muse

abundance

tradition

folklore

authentic

carousel

unique

combat

valor

hospitality

grace

www.ingramcontent.com/pod-product-compliance
Lightning Source LLC
Chambersburg PA
CBHW041153070526
44584CB00004B/291